To be free of fear is exquisite.

Rag Doll

Rag Doll

A Journey of Healing and Integration

by

Alayna

With an *Afterword* by
Judith A. Goren, Ph.D.

Mystic Moon Publications
1997

First Edition.

ISBN 0-9658490-0-7

Library of Congress Catalog Card Number: 97-72778

Cover Art: *Spiritual Journey* by Alayna ©1995.

Cover Design: Michele Montour

Colleges, Universities, Professional, and Non-profit Organizations: Quantity discounts for this book are available for educational purposes or fund raising. For further information contact: Mystic Moon Publications, P.O. Box 252032, West Bloomfield, MI 48325-2032.

To my husband,

my son,

my daughter

Acknowledgements

To each of my dear friends, I could not have finished this without you.

D., you've been a sister to me since the beginning. I'm grateful for our special friendship. *R.,* you were the first to read this. Your kind response and your complete acceptance of me melted my fears away. *F.,* I know how hard it was for you to read this. You knew me since my birth, and you cried when you read about my childhood. Your constant hugs and love kept me going. *K.,* you were so warm and accepting after reading my manuscript, you gave me the courage to continue. *N., L.,* and *L.,* without your loving encouragement, *Rag Doll* wouldn't be in existence today.

Each of you in your very special way gave me courage and strength after I shared with you my most intimate past. You didn't judge, you didn't condone; you simply gave me your love and support. I'm forever grateful to each of you.

Judith, words inadequately express my gratitude. You were by my side throughout my painful journey. Just when I thought I could go no further, your encouraging support kept me focused. Your gentle persistence and reassuring guidance helped me heal. How can I ever thank you?

To my husband and children, your loving hearts, caring words, and magnificent strength not only helped me heal, but gave me much to look forward to. We have a wonderful lifetime ahead of us. Thank you for your unconditional love.

June, 1997

Introduction

My real name is not important. It is far more important to tell the true *facts* of my life. I am not ashamed, angry, or disappointed with my life. I just feel it is unnecessary to bring a complicated and unwanted burden to my family and their loved ones by using my real name. My life is mine. My story is mine. I hope that you, the reader, will understand and feel what I felt, see what I saw, heal as I healed.

This book began from a series of letters I had written to a friend. Its sole purpose now is to help others. The more our society knows about child abuse and its repercussions, the sooner it will stop. Children become targets, victims, and possibly abusers themselves because adults, in an unthinking state of mind, act violently against them while they are still young and innocent.

This book is not intended to hurt, defame, or accuse. It is simply my journey of healing. I was blessed with wonderful helpers, supporters, loved ones, and friends. I pray my words can instill hope and encouragement in other people who have a journey to travel similar to mine. My intent is simple. I hope my words will be heard by the abused, the abusers, their loved ones and therapists.

This violence must stop. Children *do* remember.

Rag Doll

As I open the dust-covered wooden toy box,
I see the crumpled rag doll.

She's entangled in a mass of string.

Now I see...

she's only a puppet.

Letter One

Dear Nancy,

I can't believe we've known each other for over eighteen years. Even though you moved away five years ago, I still think of you as my best friend. I'm writing to you instead of calling because it's easier for me to share certain feelings with you in a letter.

I haven't been telling you everything that has happened to me at home over these past few years. When we have talked to each other, sometimes I couldn't answer your questions because personal matters were clouding my feelings. At times you seemed upset... not angry, just confused. It's okay. I understood your confusion. I didn't have the courage to explain everything to you then, but I do now.

When I recently told you the tumor on my thyroid gland was malignant, I heard your sorrow. Don't worry, I'll be fine. I also heard your gasp of surprise when I blurted out the timing was ironic because for thirty-nine years part of me didn't want to live, and now all I *do* want is to live.

I must admit it's been hard for me to understand why this tumor grew inside of me. I have finally healed after years of emotional turmoil... only to find out I have cancer. It doesn't make sense. All my years growing up, I really wished I were dead. Now I think someone is playing a joke on me. I know I'll be fine. It's only thyroid cancer and it's totally curable, but it is a nuisance. It's also a wake-up call.

I have been silent my entire life; perhaps I created my own blockage in my throat. Now that the cancer and blockage have been removed, it's time for me to speak.

I sense that anything I tell you probably won't surprise you. I know you are a caring, warm person, and you won't pass judgment. I would feel uncomfortable if anyone read or heard my story and was shocked. What happened to me is not important except that once I remembered my past, I was able to go forward and heal. If others can benefit from my journey of healing, I will share it with them.

On April 9, 1992, I was in the midst of a heated argument with my fifteen-year-old daughter. I don't even remember what it was about. All I knew, then, was that her harsh words sounded familiar. Suddenly, I felt explosive emotional pain inside as I heard and felt words from my childhood, cutting me apart like a knife slicing though me. I felt I was a horrible person. Everything was my fault. I was bad. I was a burden to my family, and a terrible wife and mother. I took an overdose of *anti-depressants* (ironic, isn't it?). I didn't think I was going to die; I just wanted to stop the pain.

When I awoke in intensive care, I was quite surprised. I looked up from my bed, saw all these tubes connected to me, and laughed when I saw a tiny red light bulb taped to my index finger. I looked like ET with his red finger. When I told the nurses, they laughed explaining that this simple device let them know if I had enough oxygen in my blood. At this point, they told me I had come into the hospital near death. I felt terribly ashamed. My daughter was white with grief, pain and sorrow.

I stayed in intensive care a few more days. I thought I was doing fine physically, but the doctors were afraid I might have a heart attack because of the medication I had taken. Emotionally I felt much better, except when I felt guilty for the stupidity of my self-destructive act. I'll never forget the different women that stayed with me around the clock while I was in intensive care. They were called "sitters." Their job was to sit and watch over the patients who had attempted suicide to make sure they didn't try it again.

The first night, my sitter was a warm and compassionate woman who told me how much my family loved me. She made me feel everything would be fine. The daytime sitter was cold and judgmental. Believe me, that was the last thing I needed. I felt bad enough as it was. Fortunately, the next night sitter was a sweet young woman. We talked and laughed for hours. Finally she looked at me and said, "Please don't take this the wrong way, but I don't understand why you wanted to die." I couldn't answer. I wasn't angry or upset – I didn't know the answer myself. I realize now, for me to try to kill myself, I must have been in horrendous pain. When the doctor asked me if I wanted to go home, I told him emphatically, "Yes!" I also told him about a fantastic dream I'd had. I hardly ever dream, but this was so real I couldn't stop thinking about it.

I was floating extremely fast in some gray misty area. I was frightened because I didn't know where I was or what was happening to me. I couldn't stop! I just kept whooshing through this grayness toward a small light. Some figures approached and I recognized my young cousin who died when she was fourteen. We were very close; she was like a baby sister to me. I felt her love, laughter, and sincere happiness. She communicated her feelings without speaking. I felt calmer. I tried to envision her as she would have looked at age thirty, since that's what her age would have been had she not died.

There she was giggling and laughing, and as loving as she was at fourteen.

I saw another deceased cousin's presence. I never really knew her when she was alive, but in what seemed like a second, I felt we were one. She communicated her feelings without speaking. I felt her love. She had loving messages for her parents.

Finally, my grandfather approached me, and he kept apologizing – communicating that he was sorry and to please forgive him. I thought it was because he had been so mean to my mother when she was growing up. According to his heritage, women did not count. Only his sons were important.

Within what seemed like seconds, I was in the presence of a bright and magical energy. I felt a Love and Light that was pure magnificence. The feeling penetrated every molecule of my body. It was the most exquisite unconditional love possible. I felt totally secure and enveloped in this cocoon of pure love. I received the name of this energy as "Universal Entity of Light and Love." (It's easier to say, "God.")

While in His presence, His energy infiltrated mine. Together we looked into an object I can only describe as a pedestal holding up a crystal viewing area. It was like looking into a huge bubble. It was far more intense than watching television. Everything I saw was three dimensional and very real. I saw and felt everything I had done in my life. I kept thinking, "So that's why... Now I understand." God communicated to me that He does not pass judgment on us. We judge ourselves. We see, we feel everything that another person we are talking to (or doing something to), sees and feels. We know whether our words or actions are painful (or loving) because we FEEL all that person feels.

I was given the choice to stay or return and realized I wanted to return to my husband and children... especially my daughter. Before I could get the full thought out, I felt myself being "whooshed" away. I awoke gasping, as if someone had just smashed a fist into my abdomen knocking all of the air out of me. It was so real. All I knew then was that I was grateful to be alive.

I couldn't wait to leave the hospital. My husband, Michael, drove me home on a beautiful sunny day. Though I've driven on this street many times before, on this day it looked and felt different. Trees lined the road. Busy cars rushed by as usual, but the colors and sounds were intense. I removed my glasses and could still see the crisp vibrant colors popping out at me. It was as if I was seeing and hearing everything for the first time.

When I arrived home, I was happy and calm. After many hugs with my children, I decided to lie down. Immediately, it felt like a warm blanket was surrounding me, as if I was wrapped in my mother's arms. It was comforting and reassuring. I slept peacefully. This feeling continued for many evenings to follow, but as the days progressed, the intensity began to dissolve. I wanted this loving, warm, cocoon-like feeling to continue forever.

Days passed and I kept remembering the strange dream. I didn't understand it. I felt compelled to go to the library to search for answers. It was such a strong desire I couldn't ignore it. Once I arrived there I looked for books about "near death." I guess it was because the nurse had told me that when I came into Intensive Care, I was very "near death." I found Raymond Moody's book, *Life After Life*. I began reading it, then I began shaking. I couldn't. No. I didn't want to believe that this had happened to me. It was <u>too</u> unbelievable and frightening. I'd had a classic Near-Death Experience (NDE).

I had a very difficult time accepting that I'd had an NDE. The description in Moody's book explained most of my dream, but it was so unlike my prior thinking to believe this kind of experience. My background and beliefs had always been, "I'll believe it when I see it!" This was not concrete or tangible; this was a dream.

I then read another book from Time-Life Library on "psychic phenomena." As I began reading their description of a near-death experience, I told my family that it was silly. They were glamorizing it and sensationalizing it. It still didn't seem possible to me. Then I turned the page and my mouth opened in disbelief. There was the picture of the gray misty area where I had been floating and I had seen my cousins and grandfather. I sat completely stunned and told my family, "Oh my God! It did happen!" This was so hard for me to believe and understand, yet others had had the same experience. I had to believe what happened to me was true. I'd almost died.

After accepting my near-death experience, I began writing a journal. Unusual things happened to me, such as waking up in the night and finding myself in unusual positions which, I found out later, were yoga. (I'd never studied or known anything about yoga.)... Then I felt this tingling in my hands, and my computer stopped working. It was brand new and the company kept checking it. The repairman couldn't understand why it had stopped... The worst thing happened when I felt a warm energy in my hands. I went to turn on a light switch, and not only did the bulbs blow out, but so did the whole track and the switch. (Later I found out that this is a somewhat common phenomenon with NDErs.)

Anyway, I'm telling you about the NDE because I feel that, when I was reviewing my life, I retained some of my childhood memories. I remember seeing my life and the feeling of complete understanding, but I did not remember the exact details of what happened to me during my lifetime. As I look back at some of my early journal entries, it is quite amazing to see some of the things I wrote.

5/13/92 I feel like I'm running away from something. I don't know what it is. Do I have to remember my childhood to get better emotionally? Am I dwelling on it too much? Am I trying to fool myself that things weren't so bad? What's going on? What am I hiding? Am I hiding?

I haven't been real warm to Michael or the kids for the past day. I know that he is scared and trying, but I don't know myself what is going on. I know I'm expecting my period, but give me a break – I can't blame everything on my menstrual cycle. I have lots of questions. Where and when do I get answers? What if they are too painful? I find it difficult to talk to my parents because I'm angry and feel sorry for them. I have to pretend that everything is fine. I don't think that letting them know my problems will accomplish anything. They didn't know any better. But it is still hard for me. I can't dwell on it, yet I keep going back to IT.

What is IT? Why am I so afraid to think? Why am I so afraid to remember?

It looks like I have work to do. Help. I hope that I have enough inner strength to pull through this. Once I do find some of the pieces to this puzzle, I hope I will fit together. That will be nice. There is hope. I won't give up. Maybe my fears are silly. Maybe nothing happened.

Denial.

Months passed. I wrote more in my journal. More interesting things happened. Much of it was metaphysical, which was like a foreign language to me. I'm very spiritual now. I KNOW God exists and I'm no longer afraid of death. I must admit, as I was getting my memories, I wished I had not come back from death; the pain of remembering was so intense. But everything happens for a reason.

I went to a Seminar on September 12, 1992, just before the Jewish holidays of Rosh Hashanah and Yom Kippur. It was lead by a Rabbi, and he was supposed to be very spiritual. I am not very religious... spiritual yes... religious no. I went.

Once there, I didn't know anyone. As I looked around the room I didn't know what to expect. All I knew was that I felt safe. One young woman asked me why I was there. I told her I didn't know except that I'd had a near-death experience five months earlier. I wanted to be with spiritual people. Her father had died recently, and she wanted some answers if I could help her. She was concerned about the way her father died and whether he had died in pain. I told her what I had learned, that once we leave our bodies, we do not feel any pain. I told her about my experience of the beauty of the other side and God's pure unconditional love. She felt relieved. I promised myself then that I would not speak of the experience the rest of the time. I was there to learn, not to discuss my NDE.

We gathered in a circle. There must have been forty of us. Some knew each other, but most of us were strangers with the common goal of wanting to be there. As the hours passed and we did visual meditating, I was at peace within. Suddenly the thought came: "God, I will not speak about the NDE unless you ask me to." Instantly, the Rabbi asked if anyone had had a "near-death experience." Right on cue. As I raised my hand, I prayed for help to find the necessary words that would help others.

I don't remember what I said. All I remember is that I closed my eyes and relived my experience. I felt the Light, and I felt the Love again.

As I opened my eyes, others were crying, smiling, thanking me. I couldn't accept their thanks because I had not done anything other than tell what had happened to me. I trembled as I sat in my seat, grateful for the near-death experience, but not wanting recognition for relaying it to others. I was not special. I was just like everyone else.

After the conference I felt warm, whole, loving, and forgiving. I looked forward to the days to come.

Two days later, I went to the first session of a class on healing the inner child. I had signed up for this a month earlier. I felt this was great. I could take it on. I was going to go, and meet some new people and work on my "inner" self. Apprehensive, but calm, I went to the class Monday morning (Sept.14, 1992). At first it was okay. I felt I was fine. I could handle anything now. I even shared my innermost secret: I had tried to commit suicide. They were the first strangers I'd ever told. It wasn't as hard as I'd thought it would be, but I did feel the shame all over again. They accepted me.

As I listened to their problems, I felt terribly uneasy. Finally I told them I was shaking, nauseous, and had a terrible headache. They said it was a migraine, and I was holding in anger. I didn't know what they were talking about. I'd never had a migraine before. What inner anger? Why had I even gone to this class? I was stupid and I wanted to get home. Someone said to ask for "gentle persuasion." Now I knew they were nuts. Get me out of here. It was too soon to tell my innermost secret! Happy-go-lucky me had blabbed too much again.

By the afternoon, I'd tried aspirin, lying down, and total peace and quiet, but the pain persisted. I called a friend and told her about the headache. She said to ask for "gentle persuasion." AGAIN – GENTLE PERSUASION! What does that mean!

Rag Doll

By ten o'clock I was miserable. I told Michael I was lying down with the soft light on. "I'm finally going to ask for gentle persuasion. I don't know what is going to happen. Please stay with me." He lay in bed next to me. I calmly prayed and asked God, "If there is something that I'm supposed to know, please guide me with 'gentle persuasion'."

Then, as if I was in an old movie, I saw little legs in front of me. They had black shoes and white socks. Wait a minute – they were my legs, but I heard a little girl talking. "No. Don't." Michael went to grab my arm. I pulled it away. Suddenly I opened my eyes - in shock. He'd molested me; it was my grandfather. I screamed! I cried. I jumped out of bed! I paced the floor. NO! How could he! I was only TWO! Oh Lord, I knew I'd wanted to know all the stuff that had happened, but please, anything but this!

Michael held me as I cried and shook uncontrollably. Thank God he was with me. He told me tearfully that he saw me being molested. When my eyes were closed, my legs were up in the air in unbelievable contortions that I would never have been able to do otherwise. It frightened him. It angered him. He felt lost and didn't know what to do. Thank God he was with me.

Now what should I do?

My headache was gone.

That was the beginning of my memories. Many more were to follow. I was fortunate to find a wonderful doctor for psychotherapy. She made me feel safe in her office and helped me through the healing process.

I say it calmly now, but I must admit it was terrible when I remembered the abuse. I didn't want to believe it had happened to me. First denial... then anger... then acceptance. My work had truly begun. Never, in a million years, would I have believed that someone I was so proud of could have done this to me.

The dam broke and many, many more memories came. The pain was unbearable. Actually, pain is what often triggered the memories. It got to the point that, whenever I would get a headache, I knew another memory was coming. I was afraid to go to sleep at night or go to the doctor's office for therapy. I finally prayed for the headaches to slow down.

It was wondrous to see how my mind protected me in my childhood. The pain inflicted on me was so great that I shut down. I did not remember any of my childhood until these memories came through. Suddenly I was awake. I realize we are given only what we can handle. If I was aware or remembered these memories after their occurrence, I know I would not have survived my childhood. You see, I also found that out my uncle and my grandmother had hurt me as well. It sounds worse than it was because it wasn't daily, it wasn't constant, but it was enough to affect me for my entire life. Now I know why I hated myself so much. I thought I was a bad person. All of it was my fault. But let's be real... this happened to me from ages two through eight. How could it have been my fault? All I knew is what they told me.

There's more, but I think that's all for now. Yes, the memories were terrifying, and I wish they had never happened... but they did happen. The fact that I now remember my childhood is wonderful. I no longer live in this void. I finally remember the many good things that happened too.

I look forward to the future. I'm not afraid of the unknown. I look forward to new events, new people, and new places. Who will I meet? Where will I go? I feel like a child who eagerly anticipates a new morning. How sweet to recapture my lost innocence.

Letter Two

Dear Nancy,

I didn't know what to expect after sending you my last letter. I must admit I panicked afterward. I wished I could fit in the mailbox and retrieve it. I'm glad you responded the way you did.

I know I would have compassion for someone else if this had happened to them, but that's just it. It usually happens to someone else. I couldn't believe it was me this time. Please understand, after telling you, I felt very vulnerable. I felt exposed. I felt shame. Your compassion, caring, and not feeling sorry for me gave me strength. Thank you.

I know you couldn't understand how I was able to forgive so quickly, but it wasn't quick enough for me. As I read my journal, I saw the pain and confusion I had endured.

Rag Doll

Sept. 16, 1992 (Two days after my first memory)

I'm so tired, but I feel I must write. Why did he do this to me? I'm afraid to sleep because I don't want to remember more. I do, but I don't. It hurts. All these years I have felt like I'm BAD! No matter what I did, I felt I wasn't good enough. I could - no, I SHOULD do better - I'm BAD.

I want to understand that I was just a convenient object for his sick mind. IT WASN'T MY FAULT! He said it was my fault. Dear God, I was only two! How dare he use me and mold my mind so badly. It has affected me my whole life! I'm angry. I'm not shutting up. He knows he was wrong. I know it doesn't help to keep the anger inside. It's unproductive and painful to hold on to the anger. I want to release it. I will forgive him, but I still have to release the anger inside of me.

Weeks passed after my first memory. My parents became concerned because I was not my usual happy self to them. I knew I should tell them, but I didn't want to tell. (I realize now that was because abusers threaten children.) I was having a terrible time, and I couldn't cover the pain anymore. With tears in my eyes and heart, I told them. I didn't know what to expect. I guess deep down, I thought they would deny that it had ever happened. My mom, in a dreamlike voice, said that she remembered when she was a teenager on her back porch, my grandfather fondled her breast. I asked her what she had done, and she said she had

27

walked away. She cried. This was the first time she had ever told anyone. They believed me. It confirmed my memory.

I thought I would be relieved to know it wasn't in my mind. Instead, I mourned. I wished it had never happened. I then saw how, as a child, I had never felt comfortable around my grandfather. I'd always wanted someone else with me when I was in the room with him. Even when I was an adult, and my grandfather was in his *nineties*, I couldn't stand being alone with him. I couldn't comprehend those feelings. I thought I was so proud of this patriarch who was so successful, but I was terribly uncomfortable with him. Who knew?

In 1989, three years prior to my memories, my grandfather died. I was sad. I was with my cousins at my grandfather's deathbed. He kept looking at me and trying to say something, but I couldn't understand his words through his oxygen mask. That bothered me for a long time. I sincerely thought he was telling me to take care of my mom. Maybe it was wishful thinking. Anyway, after the funeral I had an anxiety attack. My family thought it was a heart attack because my chest and arm hurt so badly. This was a first for me. I stayed in the hospital a few days and was then released. I still couldn't understand why it had happened. Since then, I've found it is common for people to have anxiety attacks, or something similar, happen to them after their abuser dies.

After the first memory, there were more to come. My sessions with the doctor continued. They were difficult, but I felt safer in her office than at home when the memories would occur.

It took months before I began to forgive. Too many painful memories took place to be able to forgive right away. The worst part was when I realized others had hurt me as well. Then it was a flood for me, and I did everything in my power to stay afloat.

I don't know how important it is for me to tell the morbid details, other than to share with you the events which made me who I am today. I feel uncomfortable telling because I'm not trying to glorify or sensationalize these events. If I don't tell you, I don't know how you'll understand my journey. Please know when reading all of this, I do not hate the people that hurt me. I know that sounds unrealistic, but please understand, they did not know what they were doing to me. I'm sure that, in their minds, they were just acting or reacting the only way they knew how. I KNOW they didn't do this to *intentionally* hurt me. I was at the wrong place at the wrong time.

When the memories came, I did not feel this way. I hurt. I hated. I could not forgive. As time passed, I looked at my early childhood within a broader spectrum. I realized my abusers must have learned to behave the way they did from their life experiences. Unfortunately, they too must have been abused. I finally began to forgive them. Once I forgave, I was able to heal inside.

Maybe I should just tell you what it's like to retrieve a lost memory.

I'm in my doctor's office, and I feel intense pain in my arms and legs. I lie on a soft futon on the floor, surrounded by cushions. I know I am safe, but I feel terror rising from somewhere. I close my eyes, calm myself, and suddenly I feel as if I can't move. My arms and legs are immobile. My doctor asks what is happening. In my mind, I see a little girl about four years old with her hands tied to the headboard, and her legs tied to the bedposts. I look around the room, which is vaguely familiar. I ask the little girl why she is whimpering. She tells me she was bad and her grandma tied her to the bed. I envision myself helping her untie the curtain cords, releasing her. I want to hug her, but she is afraid of me. I ask her why this happened, and I see parts of a movie as if it's been shot in different scenes and is still unedited. It's in reverse order. First, I see the grandmother holding the child's hand, yelling at her and pulling her up the stairs to the bedroom. Then I see the kitchen. The little girl is staring at the cookie jar on the counter top. She can't reach it. She pulls the chair over and, as

30

she reaches for it, it falls to the ground shattering in a million pieces. She sees the reflection of light shining through the window on the shards of glass, making them look like diamonds scattered everywhere. Suddenly, the grandmother comes in, terribly angry, and says she has to get the little girl out of the way so she can clean up the mess. She hauls her upstairs and ties her to the bed.

I cry with her. I ask if I can hold her. I tell her the grandmother is bad, and it isn't her fault. She jumps on the bed angry and screaming, "Grandma is bad and SHE has to go to HER room!" I hug her and watch her smile. I realize that what is happening is a healing for this child.

Then I realize this child is me.

After a memory like this, I had to calm my emotions to make sure I could drive home, but I was drained. I couldn't wait to get into the house. I usually fell asleep for a short time. When I woke up, it was very difficult for me to realize what had happened. I cried. I mourned. I went on with the rest of my life. I couldn't let this cloud over me get to such a point that I became a victim. I REFUSED to be a victim. If I dwelled on "Oh, poor me," I would be miserable. Then I *would* be a victim. So I dealt with it as best I could.

As I worked through these difficult memories of my grandparents, I became fearful there had been another abuser. I sensed something inside, but I was too afraid to think about it. Finally, I couldn't stop the memories anymore. The last abuser was my uncle.

It's ironic. The one uncle I thought was my favorite was also my abuser. It's amazing what a young mind will do to protect a person. He used to say he was the only one who cared. Even when I became an adult, he said he would always protect my family and me. I believed him... until I remembered.

I used to think there was a huge box of toys in my grandparents' attic in their old house. For years I asked my mom, my sister, my grandmother about the toys in the closet. None of them knew what I was talking about, but I kept dreaming about them. Interestingly, though, I remember that, as a child, I never wanted to go upstairs. I was terrified of the attic. When my sister and I stayed there overnight, I would glance up the staircase, begging her to go with me, but we couldn't move. This always puzzled me.

Now I know why... I remember.

My uncle is telling me about the toys in the attic's bedroom closet. I am four. He lures me up there with him to the bedroom, promising I can have all the toys. He picks me up and puts me on the bed. I try to squirm away, but he tells me to be quiet, and no one can hear me anyway. Telling me to close my eyes, he begins looking, touching, and feeling my body. I'm terribly scared and feel helpless. My mind drifts away. I think only of the toys.

Once the memory came, I remembered the yellow room with the white curtains and the bed with the white chenille bedspread.

The closet was empty... there were no toys.

It's hard for me to write about this. I used to think I had the best family in the world. I wanted to be with everyone for the holidays. I couldn't wait to be with my cousins (safety in numbers?). I thought my uncle loved me. He was attentive and warm. I know he did love me in his own way. His illness, which is what I call it, hurt me and probably hurt others. He didn't know how much he hurt me. His sickness took over and he didn't think a young child would remember. That was the problem. He didn't think. He acted out, but he must have learned this behavior from his past. I'm not making excuses for him or any of my abusers; I'm simply stating the facts.

My sister told me numerous times over the years that I looked at everything through rose-colored glasses. She was right. I did. It was easier for me to pretend and live in a fantasy world than to see reality and feel pain.

Letter Three

Hi,

It's me again. It's 5 A.M. and I haven't slept for two hours now. I seem to wake up every morning at 3, but for some reason this time I can't fall back asleep. So here I am writing to you. I guess your reaction to my letter is still on my mind. I know I told you I would have compassion for anyone who experienced what I did, but as the once abused child, I still feel guilty telling what happened to me. I guess I'm still afraid of what people will think and the repercussions of telling.

Needless to say, I have more to tell. If you think what I told you before was shocking, hang onto your hat.

I already told you a little bit about some of the abuse and how I'd remembered it. As I was "seeing" what was happening to the little girl, I was just observing. I didn't think

34

of her as me. It felt like there were different people each time. I felt tremendous compassion for them. I felt their pain, but they were separate from me. First it was the two-year-old. Then I saw the four-year-old. Another time she was three, or five, or eight. They would tell me their names. One was SuSu, one was Baby, one was Becky, one was Rainbow, one was Lilac, and so on.

One day, feeling very nervous, I slowly turned to my doctor and asked her if I was a multiple personality. I prayed I wasn't, but she quietly shook her head yes. That's it! I freaked! No way! Oh boy, this was as bad, if not worse than finding out about the abuse. All I could remember was the movie "Sybil." I knew I didn't have it as bad as she did. This could never happen to me. I shook. I cried. I trembled. Was I crazy? Was I sick?

Denial. Anger. Acceptance. Now what!

Once I settled down, she explained to me that this is not an illness. I learned to realize it was a survival technique. My mind was a beautiful computer. When there was an overload, it shut down. It took all of the bad memories, put them in different boxes, and stored them deep inside so I wouldn't remember the pain. When I think about it, I was really very fortunate. But I must admit problems were also created. I used to forget things, places, and people... all the time. I thought I had the worst memory in the world. Each time one of my alter personalities took over, when I came back, I couldn't remember clearly what had just happened.

Amazingly though, Michael said, "That explains it." He wasn't upset. I think he was relieved. Suddenly, my moods, my memory losses, my ups and downs... made sense to him. I wasn't a bad person; I was just very creative in my survival.

The next phase of my journey of healing had begun.

This is harder to write than I thought it would be. When I began sharing my life with you I felt free inside... until now.

I didn't understand what being a multiple personality was. I had a horrible time dealing with it. I became a recluse. I stopped seeing my old friends. I thought that now that I knew I was "different," they would see right through me. How could I be with them? How would I act? Who would come out?

I was terrified. The one thing I always wanted in life was to be like everyone else. I couldn't bear being different, standing out, or not fitting in. I didn't know why. Maybe it was because I didn't remember things about growing up. I always pretended that I remembered, but I did this to cover up. I felt dumb.

I don't think I ever blacked out. I just didn't remember names, places, and events real clearly. Being a multiple explained it.

Therapy became difficult. Once I realized these memories involved different personalities, I became frightened. I didn't know what to expect. I felt helpless.

One day, as I closed my eyes, I envisioned a rag doll.

I see the crumpled rag doll. She has a terrible frown, soiled face, wrinkled clothing, dirty yarn hair, listless eyes, and string holding her body, arms, legs, head. She is crumbled in a tight little ball looking up and lost. "Please help me." She doesn't know what to do. The alters each take a string to manipulate her to life. Sometimes Tommy is the dominant one, or SuSu, or Elizabeth. Sometimes they fight to have control. When Deena takes over, terror is present in the doll's eyes. Sometimes it is a calm transition as each personality gently stands back to let another have control.

I was the rag doll.

As time progressed, I progressed. Therapy became easier. Please bear with me as I try to explain what happened to me and how I merged into this unique, whole person. Maybe I should explain this a different way.

Hi. I'd like to introduce you to my new friend. She just moved here. She's been away her entire life, but she has had numerous interesting experiences. She basically was living in a coma, but she has finally become awake. She remembers her life now, but as she was living it, it seemed to be a dream. She remembered parts of it, but she used to fade in and out of remembering.

The following may be sung to the theme song of "The Brady Bunch":

Here's the story of a little lady,
who was growing up with seventeen different names,
She thought she knew what was happening,
but she lived in vain.

Then this lady got her memories,
of a childhood that wasn't very nice.
She cried and fought within herself,
and prayed everything would be all right.

As time... went by,
she met the other people inside.
She found that they were delightful,
and they helped her survive.

Now, this little lady,
has a life that is complete.

Rag Doll

She has a loving family,

and lives her life in peace.

Okay, I'm not trying to be flippant, but I don't want to be melodramatic either.

Remember... this story has a happy ending.

Letter Four

Hi Nancy,

I'm glad you liked my song. You really are a dear for not going nuts on me. If you thought I was nervous after sending you my first letter, that was nothing compared to my anxiety over the last one. I'm sure you were surprised to hear that I was a multiple. Hey! If I was stunned, why wouldn't you be?

It was tough when I told Michael, then my parents, and months later, my children. My daughter had a terrible time. She had just seen the movie "Sybil" in school. Timing was unbelievable. She literally ran away from me into her room. Talk about compassion. My son stared at me, got very fidgety, and jumped up saying he had to have a smoke. This was a great way for me to open up. The support, the love, the caring was... overwhelming? Sure. Okay, maybe they weren't ready. But who is?

Their cold behavior hurt me. I was disappointed and angry until I realized they were young, inexperienced and frightened about multiple personalities. Even adults have difficulty with it because of misinformation, fear and preconceived opinions. I recently heard an unusual interpretation about multiples from a woman who claimed to have a psychiatric background. She felt that multiples have different entities attached to their souls that are acting out different personalities. There may be people out there that have had this problem, but they are not the same as the people who were abused during their early childhood. Her theory was so unbelievable that I realize now how imperative it is to clarify *society's* understanding about multiples. Much has to be explained.

First, we are not freaks of nature. Second, we are extremely creative, brilliant, and courageous. Third, we are not weird. Fourth, we do NOT have entities attached to our souls. Fifth, tremendous traumatic experiences happened to each of us at an early age (usually before the age of three) and continued during our childhood. Last of all, yes, we can heal and merge.

At this point, the exact details of the abuse are not necessary to explain. The main point is that when the child or infant is being tortured, the brain is trying to understand what is happening. It cannot understand the pain being inflicted upon her or him. It is too young to comprehend the abuse; therefore, it shuts down. Computer overload. The thought stays within the child, but the child does not want to remember. The brain records every memory, even horrible ones. The memory of abuse gets buried deep within. When the trauma happens, the personality that holds the pain, splits off and remains the same age as it was at the time of the abuse. This continues indefinitely or at least until the abuse stops. Different events in the person's life may trigger the pain and the different personality emerges who knows how to handle the situation. This is my interpretation. The solution for coping as an abused child really seems quite simple, yet brilliant. Each multiple is unique, as is each of his or her personalities.

When I first found out I was a multiple, I was terrified. It was horrifying. I was a freak. No. My childhood wasn't so bad. A multiple personality was a sick person. It was crazy to be different people in the same body. It couldn't be.

As my personalities began to emerge, it was frightening to me. How could it be? I don't remember my childhood that way. No one could have hurt me that badly. Then I realized I *didn't* remember my childhood. It was selective memory. I could remember a few events, but nothing bad.

Ah, yes. My mind worked well. It learned to shut down quickly. It did its job well. I became creative so I wouldn't remember the pain. I call this survival.

I don't know how to explain this in an easier way. Maybe if I tell you about my journal, my feelings, my therapy sessions, and my observations, they will make more sense. I must admit, things were not very clear for me at the beginning, but they definitely improved as time progressed and I stopped being afraid.

October 12, 1992 (One month after the first memory)

I sense the five-year-old little girl in me is still troubled. She gets quiet, depressed, and won't speak. I had memories very early Saturday morning. My body acted out more abuse. I physically felt, yes, this abuse happened, but who did it? I realized that, while this abuse was taking place, I couldn't speak. I don't know, but I'm wondering if I was an infant then. All day I seemed to be plagued with confusion and depression. I was with my husband at the store and, as I saw three little girls with their family, I wondered to myself if they were being abused. Then later that afternoon I saw more little ones and asked myself the same question. How sad.

I can't believe all of this. The doubts about relationships are so great. My childhood is one big question now. Who else hurt me? My head hurts now. I'm starting another headache. I guess another memory wants to come out.

I know the five-year-old, Little One, is having a tough time. The twin eight-year-olds (boy and girl) have each other, but they too will have to heal. I sense that there are the four of them, including the four-year-old, Baby Girl. She feels the best because she has confronted her abuser and she finally isn't scared anymore. I think she is definitely headed for recovery. Now I will help heal the others. My biggest concern is whether there are more abusers and more personalities that will come through in my memories.

You can see how fast the memories and personalities were coming out. It's as if they were finally given permission to speak, and they all wanted to be next. It was devastating. I had to ask them to slow down. It was so hard for me to listen, to feel the abuse, to find out how bad my childhood really was. I literally had to pray and ask that the personalities and memories wait until I was in my doctor's office. It wasn't just for my sake, but also for my family's sake. Then I became concerned about whether it would happen in public. Amazingly enough, my asking made it stop. I also prayed that I not feel the physical abuse. Please let me remember without reliving the pain.

This is not easy.

When I was with my doctor, I would tell her what happened during the week. Just small talk about the kids, Michael, whatever. Then I would feel a small pain inside. Usually, it was a headache, as if someone was tapping on my head. If I ignored it, then I REALLY felt the pain. It was like "Hey... let me talk. You can't forget me now."

I closed my eyes, took deep breaths, and felt like I was leaving the room. Suddenly I would hear someone speak, usually a young voice, or an angry voice, but it wasn't my voice. My body might change position. It felt like that, but I couldn't see because my eyes were closed. The voice would say something and my doctor would ask who was speaking. The voice might say its name or say "no name" until it decided what name it wanted to have. I mean, it was fascinating. I say that now, but I sure didn't think that then. I'll never forget when Deena first came out. Her voice terrified me. She screamed and was always angry. She really wanted to protect me. She felt if she had been around when I was little, nobody would have hurt me... us.

As I got to know the many facets of my inner self, I saw them as individuals. The older alters knew the younger ones, but most of the children did not know each other. They actually met in the doctor's office. It was like having a family reunion with relatives who didn't know one another. They respected each other, as I respected them. I actually became very fond of them. They existed to protect me. They were my own personal bodyguards. When I think about it, as crazy as it may sound, I was actually pretty lucky. Once I met them, I never got lonely, and I had my own personal cheering section!

It's not been as easy as it sounds. I know I often get overly optimistic. That's my defense mechanism. If I constantly dwell on how difficult my life was as a child or even as an adult, I will smother myself in anger, fear pessimism, and depression. Then why should I bother getting up in the morning? Why bother smelling the flowers, watching the sunset, or laughing with my family? It's not worth dwelling on the negative. I'm here now, *enjoying life*, and I'm thankful every day that I was given a second chance.

$$\mathcal{L}etter\ \mathcal{F}ive$$

Dear Nancy,

You're right, it hasn't been easy. As each memory and personality appeared, I was terrified. I'd pray, please let this be the last.

I wasn't so lucky. Opening my mind was like finding a hidden treasure. First I had to dig through layers and layers of dirt and obstacles to find the box. What happens after I open this box? What will I find? Will it be empty? Will it have miraculous treasures, or just junk?

My life was in that box. But what life? I had been living in a dream for thirty-nine years. What was real to me? Who was I? I couldn't remember my childhood, events, people, or places. The people I thought I knew were really false. They'd hurt me. They'd tricked me. They'd abused me. Who could I trust? The foundation of my life, my being, my existence was shaking from its core. If I didn't know them, how did I know myself?

As my memories surfaced and I met new personalities, I learned more about myself.

You remember my memory of the little girl tied to the bed? That was my first experience having communication with one of the abused children. Don't forget I didn't know I was a multiple then. In my mind, I saw a four-year-old child crying, spoke to her and comforted her. She said her name was SuSu. My doctor asked how could I make her feel safe. I asked within what could be done to help her. I saw myself as an adult go to her in this dreamlike state, hold and hug her. I loved her desperately and let her know it wasn't her fault. The adults were horrible monsters who'd hurt her, and they will never hurt her ever again. I saw her cry and look at me, but she still doubted me. I asked her to go to a safe place that she knew. She didn't know of any place she could go. How pathetic. She never felt safe!

In a dreamlike state, Angelique, a beautiful childlike helper, came. After each memory, she would come to the little one, be it Baby, SuSu, or Becky, and take her to the beautiful field of wildflowers. At first, each was afraid and shy. Then other children would come to the one who was hurting, hold her, love her, and let her know she was safe. They ran. They played. They laughed and tumbled in the flowers. It was the first time they ever laughed and felt safe. What joy it was to see them happy. They knew no one would ever hurt them again.

They began to trust me and know my love for them. I know this may sound unusual. I am talking about them as if they were individuals when in reality they were parts of me. The difference in this is that I didn't *feel* that they were me. It's as if I was talking to someone on the telephone. I communicated with them even though I didn't see them. I sensed their presence and saw them in my mind. There was a definite connection... just not physically.

They became very real to me. They were *finally* given permission to speak... to be angry... to be acknowledged.

We built a strong sense of trust, protection, and love. This is why it was difficult for me to tell anyone about them. I saw them as individuals who were not only friends but also family I had to protect. I did not want to betray their trust. For their entire existence, they had not been allowed to speak. They had been in fear of retribution from the abusers. In my heart, I made a pact with them to keep them safe. When I began to speak about them, I felt I was breaking this pact. I was telling their secrets.

I didn't want to tell. I couldn't speak of the pain, the abuse, or the violation. I was frightened for them, and for myself. The words, the fear, and the anguish were lodged in my throat. My silence created a blockage. My silence created a malignant tumor. The malignancy has been removed, and I am no longer silent. I am not afraid. My words are flowing freely now.

I realize I was not betraying them. I was not telling to be vindictive, shocking, or to sensationalize my life. Just the opposite. I've never felt comfortable being the center of any attention. My life has been private. I used to... and still do... wish I could be a fly on the wall and observe life as it is happening around me. This is not judging, this is observing. I am finally learning about life, people, and relationships. I've been asleep for a very long time, but now I am awake!

Letter Six

Hi,

Okay, Nancy, I know you have many questions. That's to be expected. I did too.

As time progressed, I became more comfortable with each of the personalities. I realized that they were me... I was them.

11-7-93

My name is Shoshana. My name is Becky, SuSu, Elizabeth, Heather, Chest-hurts, Maddy, Deena, Dede... the list seems endless. These people are all a part of me. They helped me grow and become the person I am today. They protected me from harm and danger. I owe my life to them, even though one of them tried to kill us. I love them. I respect them, and I am grateful to them. We are healing and becoming one.

As you can see, I wrote that a year after retrieving my memories and finding out I was a multiple. I had a very busy year meeting new "people" and learning about myself. As I said before, each personality was unique. She (or he) had one purpose and one purpose only. This one became my bodyguard. That one became my protector. Another became the safekeeper of my soul.

It's interesting. I used to know these personalities as if they were my children or my siblings. For over two years, they were a part of my daily life. I got to know them and sense when they wanted to come out. They would speak in therapy sessions and, as I learned more about them, I helped them heal.

Now I have to strain to remember them. I thought they would always be a part of my life. Since I have merged, I realize they will always be with me because they *are* me. It's hard to differentiate or separate them now, but I feel I must explain them to you to help you understand me and the healing process.

Baby is two years old. Grandfather takes her in the garage and molests her. He picks her up, puts her on the tabletop, and probes her young body with invading hands. Her pain is traumatic. I had a very difficult time understanding her when she emerged. She was so very young that she, herself, couldn't understand what was happening to her. She was incapable of explaining the abuse. One of the helpers had to observe what was taking place and communicate the sequence to my doctor and me. I feel she was the first personality to split from me. Her sense of pain, fear, and danger had to be stopped to survive, so her mind withdrew and blocked the pain.

Becky is two and a half, almost three. She wears a navy blue knit skirt, white blouse, and blue knit sweater. The uncle makes her sit on his lap, and he fondles her. This confuses her because it feels good. She wants him to stop. She's squirming to get away, but he holds her tight and hurts her. She sees the mean monster. That's when I learned to be quiet, for fear of horrible pain. That's why I stopped wanting to wear skirts. I fought with my mother to wear long pants all the time. She never knew why... neither did I.

SuSu is four. She endures much pain. Grandmother ties her to the bed when she accidentally breaks the cookie jar. Uncle sexually abuses her upstairs in the attic. Grandfather uses her to teach his son (the uncle) to be a man. He tells the uncle what to do to her sexually. Terrified SuSu tries to run away from them, but the uncle grabs her. He doesn't want to hurt her, but the grandfather insists on using her. His son must become a man. Grandfather grabs SuSu's rag doll away from her, twisting its neck and throwing it across the room; he threatens to do the same to her if she ever tells. He lights a cigarette, threatening to burn her face if she screams or tells anyone. This explains why as an adult, during extremely stressful or frightening times, water blisters formed on my face. When I went to a dermatologist to ask for treatment, the doctor said she'd never seen anything like it before. She did studies, sent samples to labs, and tried different treatments, but she could never find out what caused them. During psychotherapy their frequency of occurrence progressively worsened until SuSu and the others were healed. The blisters have not returned since my personalities have merged.

Shakey is five. She sits on the window seat at the grandparents' house. She's looking out the window and the uncle comes up to her from behind. She shakes and trembles in fear. To this day, I get extremely nervous if anyone stands behind me or looks over my shoulder.

Rainbow is six. She is artistic and creative. She keeps us calm and happy in her beautiful world. She creates a pink and purple world of love and happiness. She loves rainbows, colors, textures, and fitting things together. She knows how to have fun and stop the pain. She never feels pain, but she's the protector of the abused. She stops the pain by creating her own beautiful environment. When the abuse was happening, I escaped. My mind shut down. I stopped the feeling. I split. I hid. I dreamt. This is when "Rainbow" emerged. When I first met her in therapy, she said she was six, but she had been around a long time. I don't know how long that could have been because a six year old's concept of time is different than an adult's concept of time. She's the creative one. She's the one who blessed me with my talent in art.

Tommy and his twin sister, Beth, are eight. The uncle makes Beth have oral sex on him when my sister and I stay at his home while my parents go on their first vacation. He molests Beth when my sister and aunt are shopping. Beth feels helpless and cries; Tommy evolves to protect her. His "tummy" always hurts from his anger toward the uncle for hurting his sister. This is the uncle that says he will always take care of us, that he's the only one in the family that cares. After he abuses Beth, he says that if it weren't for him, my father wouldn't have his job. In other words, don't tell or your father is out of work. Tommy's "tummy" hurts. He's angry and he holds the words and the pain inside to protect my family and me from harm. Now I know why I have always had stomach problems.

Sheila (She-Loves) is the one who likes people. She's happy. She feels special and likes to make others feel happy and special. She looks forward to the family getting together for the different holidays. She has no memory of the abuse. She wants to feel loved and special. She's ten.

Lilac is special like Rainbow. She's older, about thirteen. She feels motherly and protective of the young ones.

Rag Doll

She helps during therapy as the interpreter for the children. She knows most of the young personalities, but not the older ones. She is strong and helps tremendously. When it was too painful, or they were too young to verbalize what was happening, she observed what was happening to them, and relayed it to my doctor and me.

Heather, Maddy, and Deena are triplets. They came out at the same time – as teenagers. *They are thirteen, almost fourteen. Heather cries frequently. She's hurting inside from others' actions, words, innuendoes. This is not sexual. When she's angry, she cries. After the tears, Maddy takes over. She gets angry and her face shows the anger. She doesn't quite express it, but when it's really bad Deena takes over. Deena is very angry and fights verbally. She has the "big mouth." She yells. She screams.* They have been with me throughout my life since the age of thirteen.

Lola is an offspring of Sheila. She's fifteen, but her feelings began as a younger child. She enjoys lovemaking, but still gets scared. She likes the feelings at first, but the fear of pain stops her. The guilt feelings also stop her. She doesn't realize it's okay to feel good. She's terribly confused. She thinks she is bad, and all of the bad things that have happened are her fault.

Suzanne and Elizabeth are older versions of SuSu and Becky. Suzanne holds all the pain of the childhood abuse. She hates herself and wants to die all of the time. She doesn't attempt suicide, even though she wishes for death constantly. She came out at an early age, but is the same age as Elizabeth.

Elizabeth comes out at sixteen. She feels Suzanne's pain. They are very upset at home. Mother is screaming and yelling again. Mother slams the door. Father yells to keep peace at home. He knows what Mother is like. Elizabeth goes to the bathroom. She wants to kill herself. She opens the medicine cabinet. All she finds are aspirin. She stops after taking six pills, realizing aspirin won't do it. Elizabeth came out again on April 9, 1992. She almost succeeded this time.

Chester (Chest Hurts) is older. He comes out during stress. He actually evolved when I was a young adult, when tension at home, school, or work became unbearable. He really came out after my grandfather died, and I went to the hospital with severe chest pains. He did his job well. He was my "safe heart keeper."

Dede's an offspring of the triplets. When she comes out, everyone is terrified. Her voice, her actions, her physical presence are pure venom. She's so angry she becomes physical. She's extremely mean. She's in her twenties. She feels if she had come out earlier, she would have saved us from being abused. She makes sure it will never happen again. The basis for her beginning was much earlier in my life, from frustration at not being heard. She stayed in me until I married. Then she came out full speed ahead! Fortunately, she didn't emerge very often. The others tried to help her keep in control. Her voice and actions were my mother and grandmother.

Then there is Shoshana... very special Shoshana.

Each of the personalities is very important. Each has its purpose, its goal, its mission.

Shoshana is the strongest of all. When she comes out, I feel her strength. She is the oldest and the wisest. She knows all of the personalities, and she also interprets for many of them. Lilac is surprised to meet her because she thinks she is the protector. At first she didn't mind Shoshana, but as time progresses and I become stronger, Lilac feels herself weakening. It's a sad day for me... for all of us... Lilac speaks of her feelings of dying. Lilac succumbs to Shoshana to be the strong one. She knows it is best for all of us. There are tears from all of us as she weakens, and we're all grateful for her strength and protection. We know she isn't gone, but she's merging her strengths with all of our personalities.

I don't really know how to explain Shoshana. She had a presence about her, a feeling of love, compassion, and understanding. Those that were afraid to speak would frequently ask Shoshana to interpret or speak for them. She had great loving strength. Her purpose was to help me heal.

Rag Doll

She was not afraid of dying as Lilac and the others were, but she wanted to help me live knowing that they were all a part of me. Her strength gave me strength. Her calmness made me calm. Her wisdom helped me learn.

Saturday, Aug. 12, 1995

Shoshana is a beautiful name. I asked recently for the interpretation of the name. I was told it means a rose. How beautiful. To me, it means more. It means strength, encouragement, commitment, and beauty. Look how exquisite a rose is. I mean, really look inside. Layer upon layer of petals make the rose what it is. Without the layers it would be flat, without fullness, without character, just there. Its bud is tight like a fist. Then as it blossoms and begins to open, each petal is revealed. Each petal is equally important to make the rose the beauty it is. Each petal protects the core and its sweet nectar. The thorns on the stem protect its fragility from being hurt.

Yes. Shoshana is a perfect name for me. My layers of personalities made me who I am today. Each personality was equally important. Each gave me character and beauty. The thorns look frightening on the outside, but I see them as protection. When handled gently, they will not hurt anyone.

Letter Seven

Dear friend,

I know that all of this has been much for you to absorb. It must seem so unreal to you, as it did to me. I can only imagine seeing you read this. You are probably shaking your head, not so much in disbelief, but in amazement. Now, multiply your feelings tenfold, and maybe... just maybe... you'll feel a pinch of what I felt.

I have learned much about myself. Some good... some not so good. I realize I have a sixth sense. I sense what other people think or feel. I have always done this. I had to learn this to protect myself as a child. Realistically, I had to learn this to survive. I learned body language, I learned facial expressions, I learned voice inflection. I had to. Words that were spoken to me were not the truth:

"This will not hurt!" as he smiles and hurts me.

"Shut up. Don't make any noise."

"No one will hear you."

"No one will believe you."

"It is all your fault. It is because of you."

"You are crazy."

"Shut up. This doesn't hurt."

I knew when I was in danger. I knew that voice. I knew that facial expression. I knew those body movements. And he thought *I* was crazy. I was smart as a fox.

I'm glad I'm one person now, but it is still difficult at times. Memories are different. I am not as shocked. I don't cry as much, but I get angry... I remember. I REMEMBER!

For the longest time, just the mention of my uncle's name made me uneasy. If the conversation about him was too long, I would react. I reacted violently, verbally, and emotionally. I remember.

Obviously, he was the hardest for me to forgive. How could he have been so cruel? He was a monster. There is no excuse for his actions. He was an adult. How could he be so sick that he violated an innocent child? He abused me. He lied to me. He violated me. I remember!

Being whole is very different from being the fragmented person I was. I definitely see and remember differently than before. When I was in the synagogue recently, I felt a change. I used to enjoy being there with family and friends. I used to feel happy being with my cousins. I thought we were so lucky to be a family. Now I see it as a sham. It was all a lie. The pride and love I had for them was not from all of me. One of my personalities covered everything so I could survive and be with them. Now I see the actress who took care of me and responded lovingly to them. She protected me. I never would have survived being around them if I had remembered their cruelty.

I could not stay in the synagogue. I had to leave. The loving words and feelings were overpowered by the anger I had toward my uncle, my grandparents, and the family as a whole. Nobody protected me from these monsters. I had to protect myself. My personalities kept me safe. I saw the Torah. I heard the prayers. It was overwhelming. I cried. The tears would not stop. I had to leave. I was in mourning. I mourned my childhood. I mourned the death of relationships. I thought I was a happy child. I thought I was safe and protected. It's amazing what my mind did to protect my soul.

Or is it the other way around? Look at what my soul did to protect my mind.

Letter Eight

Dear Nancy,

Yes, therapy was extremely difficult. The fear of finding out what happened was paralyzing. I didn't want to remember.

As time progressed and more memories and personalities emerged, I was often too frightened to "see" what happened. After a personality came out, I was often in pain, physically and emotionally. Fear of repercussions created a paralyzing anxiety. I had to calm down to be able to cope. I had to somehow make myself and the others believe they were not in danger and no harm would come to them for revealing their secrets. My doctor asked if there was a way for me to feel safe. I then closed my eyes and prayed for help.

I see a small, but beautiful island. It's the most exquisite place in the world. As I begin walking on the beach, I feel frightened until a beautiful young woman, with long black hair crowned with a wreath of orchids, greets me. Her name is Princess Lelani. She welcomes me with love and understanding. She tells me that this is her island and no one is allowed there without her permission and guidance. She and her island will always protect me and nurture me. I slowly walk up the hill with her to a safe haven of peace. High up under the palm trees, I see the ocean for miles. The breeze of cool air, the scent of pure sweet flowers envelops me. There is a hammock between the trees gently swaying in the wind. She invites me to rest as she stands guard. As I lie cradled in the hammock, swaying with the breeze, I feel at peace. I feel safe.

Just envisioning this haven, at first, was enough. As time progressed, and more difficult memories emerged, it was not enough. One time, the physical pain I felt was so burdensome, I asked for help in healing this poor child (eight year old Beth).

I see her covered in mud from head to toe. The dirt is everywhere and she feels the weight of this horrible filth all over her. She goes to the safe island. She is terrified. She cries from the pain of the dirt's weight on her. The princess takes her to a special beautiful pond. There are exquisite flowers and birds everywhere. The water is cool, and crystal clear. There is a waterfall that sparkles like diamonds, creating rainbows everywhere in the sky. Princess Lelani holds her hand and gently takes her into the water. She begins floating and lets the princess sprinkle the healing water on her. They approach the waterfall. She stands under it and as the water falls about her, her tears freely fall into the pond. Suddenly she sees some of her skin. The dirt is being washed away. Her hair becomes lighter in color. She feels the weight disappear from her shoulders. She feels CLEAN. She feels PURE. She feels HEALED.

As I open my eyes, my tears too, are falling freely. I feel CLEAN. I feel PURE. I feel HEALED.

Letter Nine

Dear Nancy,

I was blessed with a creative imagination. I know this was my survival, but it was still very difficult for me to heal the little ones inside of me. My inner helpers were magnificent. By creating a safe environment for healing, I was able to merge quickly. My memories began to appear in a different way.

Sept. 14, 1994 (Two years after my first memory)

I feel another memory coming. This one is different. Please help me see this memory calmly. I see and feel this child's pain. I see it is me. I feel "MYSELF" as a two-and-a-half year old child. I feel the confusion. I see the tapestry carpet on the floor. I feel myself on his lap. I hear the whispers that this is "our" time. He whispers loudly in my ears to be quiet and not cry. I am frightened. I feel myself freeze and withdraw into emptiness – I FEEL MYSELF SPLIT! I am no longer in my body – my body just exists. I feel no pain. I don't see anything. I don't feel anything. He lets me go into the kitchen. My mom and grandmother are there preparing the food for the family for the Rosh Hashanah meal after synagogue. I am too little to go, so I'm with them at my grandparents' home. My uncle is there too. Mom and Grandma have to cook... They are glad that I'm so quiet and being such a good girl. They give me a cookie. (If they had only known.)

This memory was different than my others. *I was actually there.* I wasn't observing others. I saw myself as I was as a youngster. This time, I was me! I asked Shoshana to interpret the memory, but she faded away. I felt her melt into the others. I WAS AWAKE DURING THE MEMORY! I was able to see the dark, massive dining room table. It was ready for the relatives to come back from synagogue, set with the lace tablecloth, the good china, the silverware, and the sparkling crystal goblets. I saw the bright yellow kitchen, the library with its big windows opening to the backyard, and the deep burgundy tapestry rug on the living room floor. Everything was clear.

I asked the other alters to come out. They wouldn't. They smiled and said they were leaving, but they were part of me now. They SMILED! I wasn't afraid this time. I felt

67

myself growing stronger inside. I KNEW they were me! I knew that each of their characteristics was a part of me, and I could draw on them at any time. I no longer needed to fear that I couldn't handle myself. I saw their figures fade, melt, and blend together as they waved and smiled. They were not afraid. They knew they weren't dying... they were merging with me. We became ONE!

The memory itself wasn't as important to me as others had been in the past (but I did learn why I become so nervous before the holidays). The way the memory came to me was extremely important. I knew that during therapy, in the prior few weeks, some of the personalities were fading into each other. We talked about it in therapy. Some were weakening and others were strengthening as they merged. I was afraid to lose the others... afraid I wouldn't survive without them. This time I felt them say I should, and could, handle this memory. Shoshana wouldn't come out. She faded away, and I watched and felt the memory, but this was unbelievably different than any of the other memories. I didn't start crying! I didn't react to the memory; I reacted to the feeling of me leaving my body... of <u>not</u> feeling... of walking or drifting into a void. There was complete silence and calm. I saw and felt what I did to survive the abuse during my childhood. I felt myself split. I felt myself become the robot. I felt myself learn how to survive. I never wanted to remember the pain. I enclosed the memory and buried it deep within. My alters held the pain to protect me. I was afraid to lose my protectors, but they smiled and held me close as they merged within me.

April 17, 1995

My doctor asked me today about my memory at age eight. I was at my uncle's house. I was ME! I saw myself as me. I know that was when Tommy came out, but this time it wasn't me watching a slow-motion movie. This time it was me seeing my childhood! It was so different than other times. I didn't feel separate watching a memory. It was me walking through the house. I remember the pink kitchen, the stairway leading to the basement, the side door opening to the driveway. I REMEMBER! I didn't have any abuse memories; I just remember when my mom dropped us off at his house. I remember where we slept, the layout of the house, my sister being the Big Sister. I remember!

So this is what it is like to be "one." This is how people remember their childhood.

Amazing.

Being at peace is the greatest gift one can enjoy.

Sometimes the pain from memories is too difficult to endure.

Adults, even trusted relatives, can act with blind ignorance, creating lifelong pain for innocent children.

Even though I am whole, it doesn't mean the pain is gone. Different things still trigger uncomfortable feelings. The difference is: *now I am awake.* I feel the discomfort. I feel the emotions. Anger is instant. Reactions are instant. I'm learning the difference between the various feelings. I have tried to suppress some of the anger, saying that my abusers didn't know any better. I actually felt a little one inside feel the helplessness, the frustration, the abandonment. I haven't gone into myself in a long time. I thought they were all gone.

Monday, May 8, 1995

I've been feeling anxious all week. I couldn't figure out why. Today in therapy I finally went into myself and saw SuSu alone in the field. When asked if she wanted to come out, she said no, but she would communicate her abandoned feelings. I had to validate her pain and acknowledge her feelings. My constant referring to my abusers not knowing any better and saying I didn't hate them or feel angry anymore made her feel alone, unloved, unimportant. Her pain did happen, and I have to recognize it is MY pain. I have to deal with the pain appropriately and not keep saying that everything is okay. I don't have to be bitter, nor do I have to make this the only thing in my life. Yes, it happened. Yes, it's okay to be angry. Yes, it's okay to forgive, but only when I'm truly ready.

Rag Doll

I know it sounds confusing that I still saw SuSu. This surprised me too. I realized that even though I had merged, I was still in a state of transition. I had been forgiving, but for the wrong reasons. I just wanted to put everything to rest. I was lucky they were still watching over me. They helped me see... and feel. Then I was truly ready to heal myself.

SuSu feels relieved and at peace. She turns away and fades into the field of flowers.

Letter Ten

Dear Nancy,

    Yes, it has been interesting, hasn't it? Each day brings me a new adventure. Some days are fun, some aren't. So far, I've painted everything very optimistically. I think that's a bit unrealistic. The transition was, and still is at times, difficult.

    Thursday, May 11, 1995

    Pain comes in all forms. Physical, emotional, spiritual. Confusion, indecision, lack of self respect...

    My changes have been drastic. Not knowing who I was at any given time, I thought I was fine, but I was confused. Confusion is a terrible feeling. You think you know what is happening, but you're not really focusing, not sure if something really happened. Sometimes you forget instantly, then you're constantly being reminded. At least I'm whole now, but it is difficult. I feel like a child learning how to walk.

I'm unstable on my legs. I want to learn to walk faster, but I'm afraid I'll fall. What do I do next? Take a step, or plop down to get my bearings?

First I'll plop, then I'll take a step.

Much has to be learned.

Much has to be taught. Loved ones, patients, therapists, and society must learn and be made aware of the pain that children suffer at the expense of adults.

Children remember.

Children feel.

Children escape.

Children survive.

<u>Children remember.</u>

Some continue the pain as adults. Some inflict the pain on themselves. Some inflict the pain on others. Some are blessed by splitting and surviving.

When one splits and becomes a multiple, he/she is not alone. The soul has many aspects and they keep the multiple company. I repeat, this is a survival technique. I just shut down and someone else was there to take over in stress, in abuse, in art, in lovemaking, in life. In many ways, it was easier. I could be with many and never feel afraid, yet the inner turmoil was great because I didn't know who I should be until the situation arose. I guess that's why I've always been afraid of new environments and situations. I was fortunate, though: when the stress came up, so did the personality who could handle it. Sometimes some of the personalities were wonderful, other times they weren't... especially Deena. She reacted from gut fear. She attacked verbally with raw vengeance. She was frightening, but that was the only way that she knew how to protect us and survive. She was sorry she wasn't with us when the abuse first started. If she had been, she would have stopped it from happening. That's why she yelled so violently... to make sure it would never happen again.

Yes, the transition has been difficult. I think I am better. I know I am. The difference is, I now know when I am angry. It is *me* responding. I know I don't yell nearly as much as I used to, but I do react. I have to be very frustrated to get to the point of yelling. Recently, my son told me how he hates it when I yell. At first I was upset when he told me this, but then I realized that he, too, has lived with my yelling all these years, as I did with my mother's and grandmother's. I'm actually glad he told me. Now I'll do everything in my power to be calm. I also realize his body language, his shouting, his anger triggers mine. He acts like my mother and grandmother. He learned his behavior from me.

When I speak of transition, it may be confusing. I am whole now, but I am still learning. I am an adult, but like a foreigner in a new land. I am learning the culture, the people, and the customs. I observe constantly. I look at my parents, grandparents, sister, aunts, uncles, and cousins now. I knew them or I saw them differently as a child. I made them godlike in my eyes. Now I see them as human beings. I see how people develop. I see how love, anger, hate, compassion, and coldness evolve and pass from one generation to the next. At first, I had only anger for my abusers. Now I see they, too, were abused and didn't know any better. The more I learn about their childhood, the more I understand what happened to me. I see what my learned behavior has done to my family. The ripple effect is amazing.

I see many changes in my relationships with others. A few months ago I was upset with my sister. I wanted her to be the person I had invented to get through my childhood. She used to say, "Take off those rose-colored glasses." I thought she was silly and cold. Now I see why she became who she did. She saw reality. I saw fantasy. It was easier for me to exist in a fantasy world and not see or feel the pain. She put up a wall. She doesn't remember all of the bad. Her sense of survival was denying it and ignoring it. My survival was denying it, ignoring it, and pretending it was something else.

I was hurting inside so badly because I felt the loss of my sister. One evening, I had a very unusual dream. I saw a funeral in my mind, but there was no body. All I saw was me mourning as figures walked by. These figures were relationships I had invented to feel love. I saw my fantasy sister walk by and be replaced with the real sister. It was sad because I really had her on a pedestal. Now I see her for who she is... not what I wanted her to be. It's okay because I like who she is. It is just the other alters, especially the young ones, wanted to keep her as the saint, the one who would save and protect me. She couldn't do anything for me when we were children... she was too young. I prefer seeing her now as the human being that she really is, not the "Savior" I wanted her to be. I thought she had all the answers. I thought she could take care of herself. I wanted to be just like her. Strong. I see now she found her way of survival differently than I did. It's okay. I love her for who she really is... not the fantasy I wanted her to be. My feelings of love within became so strong that I sensed a healing between us. She and I now speak to each other frequently and as loving sisters.

I see and react differently. My life has changed. All that I thought was there no longer exists. My perspective has changed. I look at people differently. It's almost as if I see people without their costumes on. I stand back and look at situations; I analyze, observe, and figure out my relation in the scheme of things. I'm not judging... I'm merely observing the people without their different faces, make-up, and clothes.

I see the situation as it is unfolding before me. I have taken off my rose-colored glasses. It was easier before, when I had them on. But who's fooling who? Was it really easier? I wasn't living or learning then. I simply existed and played the part of the chameleon.

To answer your question about how I felt during my change from one personality to another, picture yourself driving very slowly on a foggy, misty day. The windshield begins to cloud up. You turn the wipers on, but it only smears your view more. You don't want to put the window washer fluid on yet, but finally you have no choice. Once you do, as quickly as can be, the smeared foggy view is replaced with clarity – a crisp clean view. You still have to find your bearings where you are on the road, but you can see clearly. This is what happened to me as one personality changed to another. Sometimes it took a second, sometimes a few minutes. Other times there was no feeling of time at all. When a situation was very bad, I would go home, close my eyes, and fall asleep. I would wake up refreshed, and a new personality would be in control. Again, the pain was too difficult for me to handle, so the appropriate alter held the pain for me until I could handle it.

My alters were very special. Once I knew they had evolved to protect me, I felt love, compassion, understanding, and pride in each of them. Once I knew they were me, I felt love, compassion, understanding, and pride in myself.

Letter Eleven

Dear Nancy,

I must admit my life has been complicated, but it's better now than it's ever been. My biggest concern has been the welfare of my family. My parents and I have become closer. I was afraid telling them everything would break us apart, but they have been wonderful. They were only sorry they didn't know about the abuse, and they weren't there to protect me.

My children had a very difficult time growing up. My heart feels love and concern for them. They didn't have just one mother raising them... they had twenty. I remember when they were young and received new toys, I couldn't wait to play with them... not the kids, their toys! I'm sure it was one, or more, of the younger personalities who came out to play. Sometimes I would be Becky, SuSu, or Tommy. It must have been confusing for them not knowing how I would react at any given time. The worst part of it was that to them, I was just their Mom. I didn't look different; I just acted differently. How could they possibly understand what was happening, when I didn't know what was happening? I never knew why we lived in such constant turmoil. I'm glad we have answers now. We still have our ups and downs like many others, but we have definitely healed most of our wounds. We are a family now.

The abuse and my multiples created problems for Michael and me. Sometimes our love life was great; other times, I didn't want him to touch me. He became confused; I became angry. I didn't think it was me. Actually, I didn't know what it was. We both thought I was terribly moody. The abuse during my childhood established a pattern of fear deep in my psyche. Until I remembered the painful events, I was incapable of healing. Even now, an unexpected touch or a whisper from behind makes me jump. At least I recognize what caused the reaction, and I don't panic.

Michael has been my loving husband, best friend, and confidante. From the onset of my first memory, our relationship was in a constant state of change. The beginning was definitely explosive. First the memories... then the different personalities. We were in a state of confusion. What was difficult for me was even more difficult for Michael. At least I could "see" the memories and heal myself. He could only observe me, and sometimes, stand by helplessly. His strength became my strength. When I needed him, he was there for me. I was blessed he was as patient and understanding as he was. My being a multiple explained some of our problems, but it also created new ones. He had to learn who my different personalities were. He had to know how to speak or act with each of them. My appearance didn't change, but my mannerisms did. Sometimes it was really weird at home. Once the alters got their voices, any one of them could pop up at the most unusual time. Sometimes they would even say who they were. Talk about unwanted company! As time went by, it became easier for him, and he could tell which alter was present.

As I began healing, he saw me become stronger. Our lives became less complicated. I was calmer, which made our home and family life calmer. His strength, support and love kept me going. I don't know what I would have done without him. I don't think I could have been as strong as he was, if the situation had been reversed.

When I found out about the tumor on my thyroid gland, Michael took me to the hospital for tests. When the doctor did the biopsy, it really hurt. All the meditating, praying, and picturing myself elsewhere, didn't work. There I was, on the bed, having the biopsy needles injected and feeling every painful moment. I told Michael that I wished the alter who held the pain had stayed with me.

So this is what it's like to be "normal." I never appreciated my other personalities as much as I did when this pain was happening. They did a wonderful job for me. Sometimes I still miss them.

Rag Doll

Letter Twelve

Dear Nancy,

I know you still have questions about how I have changed. Please understand... I am still changing, and will probably continue to do so for years to come. This doesn't worry me because all of my changes have given me a passionate desire for life I never possessed before. Change for many is a frightening word, but to me, it is hopeful and encouraging.

Since the beginning, it's been very difficult for my family and me. They didn't know this "new" woman that suddenly lived with them. I may have looked the same... I may have sounded the same... but I certainly was not the same. Sometimes I would see anxiety in their eyes. Sometimes I would see confusion. They were acting the same to me, but I definitely responded and reacted differently.

83

I never realized how passive I was. I always felt compelled to please everyone else even at my own expense. I didn't count. I didn't matter. I just needed everyone's love and approval. *Don't rock the boat. Do what you are told. Smile and make everyone happy.*

Michael recently was in a playful mood and tried tickling me. I asked him nicely to stop. He tried again. I said firmly, "Please stop." Then he tried AGAIN! That was it. I exploded. I told him he had no right to touch me or do anything to me I did not want him or anyone else to do to me. It's my body, my feelings, my rights! He backed up, looked at me with a hurt expression on his face, and denied ... he actually denied... that he tried to tickle me. I began pacing, screaming, and yelling at him. I didn't know which made me angrier, the fact that he ignored my wishes, or the fact that he *denied* what he was doing to me.

Screaming only frightened him but, unfortunately, that's what I had to do to get his attention. I stopped yelling and firmly told him not only was his touch invasive, but his denial also insulted my intelligence.

This is *my* body. It has always been my body, but I didn't know it. I didn't know I had the right to stop anyone from touching, tickling, pinching, or abusing me. Different personalities took over and blocked my feelings. I had no feelings. I was the puppet at everyone else's disposal. I just slipped in and out of myself. I just existed.

The difference now is that I am "one." I am awake. I am aware of what is happening to me. I know what I want and what I *don't* want. Before, if I said no to my husband or my children, they would try again, and I would give up and just leave "myself." It was easier to disappear, let a different personality take over, and give in rather than have a conflict with them or anyone else. I thought it was my role to keep everyone happy. I was passive and let everyone else control me and "pull my strings."

My anger helped me realize this has been happening to me my entire life. I didn't think or act for myself. Other personalities took over when I had a confrontation. Now I know why this time, after I screamed at him, Michael looked at me with a confused expression on his face. I never reacted this way before. I always gave in. I never set boundaries for myself. I never really let him know what I wanted or didn't want. I said it, but I was passive. In the past, if he didn't want to hear what I was saying, another personality took over and dealt with the situation. If it was Deena, the verbally angry one, war broke out between us. If it was Heather, I cried.

Before my healing and integration, I could never acknowledge my feelings. I didn't express anger; Deena, or Maddy, or Dede did it for me. I didn't know I was allowed to say no. This time, his denial triggered my anger *because I am whole* and I was fully awake and aware. This time, when I said no, he acted the same as he has in the past, but *I* reacted differently. The *whole* me was there. *My* verbal anger came spewing out. It was *me...* not Deena.

Before I knew I was a multiple, I felt extremely anxious when I couldn't remember different events that had happened. I lived in a dream, and everything was foggy. Michael's denial about his tickling me triggered a renewal of terrible feelings of confusion. The difference was, this time, I was whole and I didn't leave myself. I *knew* what was happening. I stood up for myself. I cut the manipulative strings and I continued to stand and fight for myself. He sat back, looked at me, and his facial expression changed again. He understood. He was upset that he had hurt me; he had never meant any harm. He really and truly acknowledged my feelings and understood my anger. This was a new experience for both of us and it brought us closer together.

This past year there has been a big change at home. All of us are learning to be a family. We speak to each other calmly and we know where each of us stands. I respect my children and husband and honor them as wonderful human beings. I am proud of them, and they know it. Now we listen to each other. We didn't really have any rapport before I healed. We all blurted, screamed, and attacked each other. I was so many different people that our relationships were always different. They reacted to me depending on who I was at the time, and I reacted to them depending on the situation and which personality would come out to handle it.

Once I merged, I "grew up" and became a functioning adult. I have learned to establish my boundaries... what I like and what I don't like. Most importantly, I see each of them differently too. I see my son's and my daughter's love and compassion and what each of them has had to endure in their short lifetimes. I see their strengths and their beauty. I've learned to become a more loving mother instead of a complex machine comprised of many different parts. I was many people of different ages, temperaments, and personalities. They had many "moms" and Michael had many "wives."

It's a wonderful feeling to be "one," and to love my family, being awake with them all of the time.

Letter Thirteen

Dear Nancy,

Even though I'm one personality now, at times I still have difficulty dealing with my feelings. In your last letter you asked me why I haven't confronted my abusers. I understand your thoughts that it would probably be easier for me now since my personalities have merged. In many ways you're right, but I must tell you, dealing with my mom's family is still not easy for me.

I found out a few weeks ago about an award ceremony that was to be held in memory of my grandparents. As soon as I heard about it, I knew I wouldn't go. I used to have a good time with my cousins, aunts, and uncles. My family was very important to me, but everything has changed. My son decided to go to the ceremony. When he returned, he told me he had a terrible time because he felt left out. I had to tell him it wasn't his fault. The family is confused as to why I avoid them so much now. I can't face them.

After talking to my son, I felt like crying, but nothing would come out. I tried talking to Michael, but I still didn't feel right. I kept pacing the floor like a caged animal. Then I wrote in my journal.

I don't understand. The pain is still so great. When will it stop? I can't be around them. They hurt me. They are confused. They don't understand why I don't want to be with them anymore. I used to love this family. I used to be so proud of them and thrilled I was a part of the family. Now I don't want to see any of them.

I know my uncle still cares. He's the most confused... or he knows I remember and I don't want to see him. I can't confront him... I'M STILL SCARED. I'm still afraid of him! God, please help me.

After writing, I began sobbing. I couldn't stop crying. I couldn't catch my breath. Michael tried to comfort me, but his words couldn't help me. I finally realized I'm still terribly afraid of my uncle. Even though I am forty-two years old, I still feel like a four-year-old child in his presence. I'm terrified of him! I know he can no longer abuse me, but the pain and fear are so deeply entrenched within my mind I feel terror when I'm around him. I have to do everything in my power to hold myself up and stay strong during the time I'm with him. The fear of pain is too terrifying, so I avoid him.

I have frequently thought about confronting him, but I can't. All I keep thinking about is what he used to say:

"No one will believe you."

"No one will hear you."

"You're crazy!"

I don't think I could handle it if he started on me again. It's not worth the pain or anguish to hear his denials. Then again, what if he confessed and actually apologized? I know at my grandmother's funeral last year he tried to talk to me, but I kept avoiding him. When he finally stood next to me in the crowded room, he said our family was really mixed up and we each had a difficult childhood. Maybe he was trying to tell me in his own words that he was sorry. I don't know... and I'm too afraid to find out. If he denies it, I'll go through the pain and anger all over again. If he admits it, I'll go through the pain and anger all over again. I know what happened to me, and he does too. Then again... maybe he doesn't remember. Maybe he blocked his memory too.

A few months ago I told my aunt, his wife, that three years ago I began remembering my childhood. I told her my grandfather abused me as a young child. She was shocked and upset, but understanding... especially after I told her my mother had also been abused. I never told her that her husband had hurt me as well. It didn't make sense for her to know. I didn't want to cause any problems for her. Now my uncle keeps asking my mom how I'm doing and he wants to make sure I'm okay. I'm sure he realizes if I finally remember my childhood, then I probably remember what he did to me.

The irony of this is that I sometimes miss him. During my adult life, when my memories were blocked, I was very close to him. I thought he was the only family member who cared. After all, that's what he always told me. I felt I could talk to him and tell him everything that was happening in my life. But as I said before, everything has changed.

I guess this is one chapter in my life I will not be able to finish... at least for now.

Letter Fourteen

Dear Nancy,

I've come a long way from my past of terror, deceit, and pain. I find I am continuously learning about others and myself. It's been two years since I merged into one personality. I'm grateful for that, but I must admit I still have my concerns.

Last year I went to a new internist for a routine physical exam. Being very thorough, she found the tumor on my thyroid gland. During my visits with her, I found it difficult to explain why I sometimes couldn't recognize pain, or why I remembered some surgeries and medical ailments better than others. I hesitantly told her about my past, the abuse, the multiplicity, the healing and merging. At first I thought she should know; then I feared she might not want to be involved with a patient like me. I thought my past might seem too complicated and unusual for her, and she would be uncomfortable treating me. I was afraid to see her reaction. I worried foolishly. When I told her my concern, she was not the least bit afraid or upset. She felt compassion, understanding, and was fascinated with my journey of healing.

Sometimes I become extremely frightened after telling others about my past. I don't shout it from the rooftops, and I don't tell everyone I meet. I do use discretion, but after telling someone, I find myself days later fearful of what he or she may think. I become extremely nervous and insecure. Yet, each person I have told has been very understanding.

I must admit, I do have one friend who rarely calls me anymore. I don't know why; she won't say. The only reason she may be avoiding me is that she, too, had a very difficult childhood. Maybe my experience opened some of her wounds.

I realize my life has been very complicated, and I've had many obstacles to overcome. I will not be ashamed of my life; if it is too difficult for some people to understand my past, I think it is sad, but it is not my fault. I am happy I have come this far, but I still have much to learn.

I recently injured myself and had to go through physical therapy to heal my body. It's interesting that I had to learn to recognize physical pain. In the past my alters did a great job hiding pain from me. I also learned it was difficult for me to have a male physical therapist work on my body. Even though I logically knew he would not hurt me, my body became very tense when he touched me. I was embarrassed, but I had to request a female therapist. We knew my emotional discomfort would hinder my treatment.

What fascinates me now is that even though I have healed so much, I still have many scars from my childhood. I have to recognize these scars and what pain feels like. I see, think, and feel more clearly now. I recognize a certain feeling of internal discomfort when I'm not sure of a situation. It's like a warning or a light that goes off inside. I stop, analyze the situation, and then react. Most people do this on an everyday basis. It's new for me, but it's getting easier each day.

My feelings are my own. I have learned it's okay for me to tell someone what I like, dislike, what I see, or what I think. I feel free. I don't have to be afraid anymore; I am experiencing life.

I'm not a bad person.

Letter Fifteen

Dear Nancy,

There's no doubt my life has been a puzzle. I feel blessed and very fortunate that I have healed and integrated. Now that I am whole, I *remember* my childhood. I'm not looking at fragmented events. I see my life in chronological order. These past three years I have re-lived my early childhood, puberty, teen-age years, twenties, and thirties. I have finally reached my true age of forty-two.

I know when others look at all that has happened in my past, they may think it was a nightmare. Some may think it was unbelievable. I think it was a journey, an amazing one at that, but definitely a healing journey. I have learned not only about myself, but also about loved ones, friends, and relationships.

I was recently asked what it was like to be a multiple. All I could do was envision a mass of papers spread out on the floor, not in any special order, but as if I were getting ready to write a term paper. My notes were scattered everywhere. I knew each was extremely important, but I didn't know where to start. Slowly, I picked each one up and put them together. Each piece fell into its perfect place. The paper was complete, and it was one. Each of my personalities was a piece of paper, but now they are bound together and complete. Now I am complete. I am one.

As you know, we just finished building our beautiful dream home, and it was one of the greatest experiences in my life. As our home was being built, my new life was being built. Envisioning what a room would look like was similar to envisioning a personality. Each part of the building process was equally important, including the planning, excavating, or framing. Each personality was equally important, including the young ones, teenagers, or adults. When completed, all parts merged together to become a beautiful home; all the different parts of me merged together to make me one.

I'll never forget the first night Michael and I moved in. I couldn't stop crying. My tears of joy would not stop flowing. Michael couldn't understand. He thought it was from the happiness of completing our home. It was far more than that. It was the first time in my entire life I felt safe and at peace.

Epilogue

Dearest friend,

My last session in my doctor's office was sad and exciting. It was a farewell, yet a new beginning.

On this last day at the office, I see the crumpled rag doll come to life. This time each personality lets go of its string, and she is still standing! Her face and hair become clean; she is poised as she sees the transformation of her body. The wrinkled dress turns into a sparkling white pinafore, and her frown turns into a beautiful smile. She moves to a place of honor on the window seat, overlooking the brightly colored, exquisite meadow of spring flowers. She is safe, protected, whole, one, strong, and... at peace.

AFTERWORD

by Judith A. Goren, Ph.D.
Licensed Clinical Psychologist

I am the one Alayna refers to as "the doctor." I considered it a privilege, one which came toward the end of my own professional career, to work with Alayna. Despite severe childhood trauma and the resulting pain and confusion of her adult years, she moved quickly in her healing process. Painful though her sessions were, she entered into the work in a spirit of cooperation, which is not always the norm for patients with dissociative disorders. She worked in great depth, and, within two years, she began the integration process which she refers to as "merging" or "becoming one." Alayna's personality now combines the strength, creativity, spirituality and compassion of all her former "alters."

Multiple Personality Disorder, or MPD, became an "outdated" term about three quarters of the way through Alayna's treatment. At that time, the American Psychiatric Association renamed the diagnostic category "Dissociative

Identity Disorder (DID), doing away with a label that has been highly controversial. I prefer the original term as used in this book because it was in use when Alayna was diagnosed, and it conveys a common, though often misunderstood, meaning to the general public.

Whatever the diagnostic label, the phenomenology remains the same. MPD is a disorder in which the mind of a child, and the adult she will become, is fragmented; her memories of events are dissociated, or held in separate "compartments" of the mind. This occurs when there has been trauma which the developing personality cannot assimilate. The memory of the trauma does not "go away"; rather, it is encapsulated as an experience separate from normal, everyday, non-traumatic life events. This is a protective strategy which allows the child to grow up rather than "give up"; it is a defense, in childhood, against suicide or psychosis. However, the encapsulated trauma is not leakproof; it often spills over into ordinary life events in the form of distortion, memory loss and painful emotions, such as terror or rage, that seem to come out of nowhere. In adulthood, untreated MPD becomes a severe disfunction.

Alayna was able to heal in therapy more quickly than most, I believe, because of two helpful factors: there was no longer any suicidal behavior, and there were several very cooperative Inner Helpers.

At the time she entered therapy with me, Alayna had already reached a decision to never again attempt suicide. Her decision came when she saw, with clarity, the devastating effect her behavior had on her family, and particularly on her daughter. We reinforced this decision with a firm therapeutic no-suicide contract. In addition, we asked for the help of the stronger alters in comforting those parts inside who were prone to despair and thoughts of dying. Therefore, we did not have to spend months (or years) of therapeutic time dealing with issues of suicidal behavior, as so often happens when there is a dangerously acting-out "Inner Persecutor" alter.

A second factor that accelerated the healing process was the active presence of several Inner Helpers, who were very cooperative with the treatment and who often served as advisors to me. At times when I felt unsure of the next step, or when I wanted Alayna to hear advice from within, rather than from me, I would ask to speak to one of these Helper parts. There would follow a moment of physical shifting in her chair, a change of expression and body posture, and the alter would softly announce her name. I then asked a short, open ended question, such as, "What would be a helpful course for Alayna to follow at home this week?", or "Why is Alayna suffering this week with so many physical symptoms?". The answer was always specific and helpful. It is useful here for the reader to remember that each "part," or "alter," was a split off piece of the consciousness of one person, Alayna, and that her inner wisdom was accessible in a light trance state. When Alayna "returned," I always reviewed with her the advice that she, in effect, had given herself. Often she looked startled, then said, "Oh, yes, that's right," as if recognizing something from a great distance.

Alayna was the "host" personality, in MPD jargon. She was the part who identified with "I", the part who was known most often in the outer world. However, the world Alayna experienced was rather limited. She had difficulty with interpersonal relationships. She avoided socializing. She was often ill, and had suffered throughout her life from a long list of physical problems. At the start of our work together, Alayna was depressed, anxious and confused much of the time. She tended to want to talk about the minutiae of daily life: a trip to the mall, what to make for dinner, the insignificant details of a minor argument between herself and a family member.

However, because Alayna had begun to have memories of abuse prior to the time I had met her, this deeper material emerged early in our work together. Commonly, as Alayna was talking about something superficial, she experienced a physical sensation, e.g.: a headache between her eyes, a tightness in her chest, aching in her arms, a cough. She mentioned it briefly, then brushed it aside and went on with her saga. At this point, I intervened with a suggestion: "Turn your attention to the sensation you are experiencing and see what it might be about."

I also suggested that she adjust her position so that she felt centered in her chair, place both feet against the floor to ground her, breathe gently, and go inside herself for information about the sensation. At these moments a visible shift in her body and facial expression occurred, and one of her "alters" emerged. Usually the physical symptom was related to the past experience of that alter. For example, pain in her arms was related to the memory of being tied to the bed when she was four.

Over time, we discovered over 70 split-off parts of Alayna. A few met the definition of "full alters," having a life history of their own. Many were child-parts, each fixated at the age of a specific traumatic act of abuse. The teenagers and adults carried more dynamic personality aspects: anger, artistic talent, good business sense, a down-to-earth matter-of-fact quality, a calming presence, wisdom, and so forth. Some of the children had been created to carry a single memory, and emerged only once or twice in my office. Others, like the sharp-tongued Deena, remained active all her adult life, both protecting her and getting her into trouble. Shoshana, a wise Inner Helper, emerged frequently at the beginning to explain events that were occurring in Alayna's present life, or to tell me about alters who were not yet ready to speak for themselves.

Each "personality" was a dissociated aspect of Alayna that emerged in a state much like hypnotic trance. I did not have to do a formal hypnotic induction: the simple suggestion to "go inside" allowed her to "go under." I learned to recognize many of the alters before they announced their names, by the wonderfully plastic contortions of Alayna's facial muscles. SuSu's mouth turned down; Meanie's face held a sneer; Shoshana looked like Alayna but without the depressed expression. When a child-alter was emerging, her body curled downward, but when a spiritual, helper/alter appeared, she yawned and stretched as if to give this energy a new space to breathe. Alayna herself was unaware of these physical changes. We talked about using a video camera, but never did.

Mutual trust played a major part in our work together. All of the parts of her that had been silent for so many years learned to trust that they could safely tell their parts of her story in my office. I learned to trust that whoever, or whatever, needed to be revealed would do so, in its own time and in the right order for her.

Sometimes, especially in the early months of our work, it was necessary for me to give suggestions to slow down the process. Otherwise, Alayna began to feel "flooded" with emotions and memories, and could barely function in her present life. We made it a priority that she be able to carry on her daily activities even while this work was unfolding, and asked the inner parts who were clamoring to tell their untold tales to wait until they were in my office. This "asking" was, itself, a form of hypnotic directive.

At first, Alayna did not remember what happened when she was in trance. Later, she began to hear the conversation as if from a great distance. Still later, she reported feeling awake and present and taking in all that was said. In a pre-final stage of the work, she would often come out of the trance almost immediately, chuckle, and say, "They want me to tell you myself." Eventually, she was able to say, "They aren't there any more. They aren't separate. They are all ME."

Before I met Alayna, I had worked with other clients in various stages of dissociation, including MPD. I also met regularly with a group of psychotherapists who comprised a local study group and peer supervision chapter of a larger organization, now called the International Society for the Study of Dissociation. (ISSD). All of us had read about integration as a final step in the treatment of MPD, but none of us had seen it happen in our own clients. We wondered what we needed to do to bring about that part of the process.

With Alayna, I did not have to "do" much at all. During many sessions, especially later in our work together, I felt as if my role was to be a silent witness to her evolving process. The integration seemed to happen spontaneously over a period of several months. Some of it happened in my office, and some seemed to occur spontaneously between sessions. Whenever Alayna expressed sorrow over "losing" the other personalities, I reminded her that they were all parts of her; she was not losing, but gaining, because the strengths and memories of each one would blend into her personality, becoming part of her forever.

With the merging of her "personalities," Alayna has, indeed, emerged as a woman of strength, wisdom and creativity. She has held together through several recent crises: the death of the grandmother, an encounter with the uncle, and surgery to remove a cancerous tumor from her thyroid, which necessitated removal of the thyroid itself. She met each of these situations with maturity and dignity.

I hope, as Alayna does, that her story will contribute to public awareness of the devastating effect on children of physical, sexual and emotional abuse, while at the same time providing hope to survivors that, with help and hard work, it is possible to heal.

Additional copies of *Rag Doll* may be purchased for $15.00 (includes shipping). To order please send your name, address, and a check or money order, payable to Mystic Moon Publications at:

Rag Doll
c/o Mystic Moon Publications
P.O. Box 252032
West Bloomfield, MI 48325-2032

Colleges, Universities, Professional, and Nonprofit Organizations: Quantity discounts for this book are available for educational purposes or fund raising. For further information contact: Mystic Moon Publications, P.O. Box 252032, West Bloomfield, MI 48325-2032.